THE $20 MILLION INVESTOR BLUEPRINT

HOW AMATEUR INVESTORS CAN BUILD THEIR PORTFOLIO TO $20 MILLION

KINGSLEY LUCAS

Copyright © 2018 by TheHolyFinancier Publishing.

Get free information, articles and more at:

TheHolyFinancier.com

To The Supreme God,

To My Beloved Divine Father & Mother,

To All The Great Beings And The Teachers Who Have Lighted Our Paths,

May All Readers Of This Book Be Blessed With Tremendous Success In Investing, Abundance, Prosperity & Supreme Happiness!

Why I Wrote This Book

I am going to start off by telling you a story. This story may or may not resonate with you. But here goes. In my 20s, I came upon a stock called Matex International, which was a publicly listed company in Singapore. Soon after I bought it, the company rallied some 60% in a matter of months. As wide eyed and eager to learn as I was then, I wished that I had the wisdom to be able to discern and fully put into use a strategy that was discovered by one of the fathers of value investing – Benjamin Graham.

Now, at the time, like many investors who start out trying to be a value investor, I too looked into Warren Buffett's idea of buying a moated company, looked at sustainable high return on equity numbers and also made a supreme effort to establish that a company does indeed have a competitive advantage that would cause its earnings, cash flows and dividends to grow over time.

That idea sounds elegant but in reality, that is one of the toughest ways to earn money in the stock market these days, especially for an amateur investor. I am not saying that you can't make money trying to identify a company with a competitive advantage but generally, it would be a long shot for most amateur investors. For one, the latent biases within us and our mental make-up cause us to come to a conclusion too soon, too quickly. That is the first conclusion bias at work here. And the other thing is that amateur investors tend to have a worldview that does not make for successful investing in moated corporations.

Perhaps, one example of that is the projection of a trend to a few years of earnings and naively believing that earnings will continue to grow indefinitely. There are just too many variables for an amateur investor to make a good return from the market. And what I mean by that is, as an investor, one should beat the market. If not, that investment operation would have been really a waste of time - your precious time that is.

I mean I like the old man, Warren Buffett but, I am going to say categorically that I have not reached the utopian situation of having a punch card where one punches 20 holes that represents 20 investments that one would make over his lifetime. I am not Warren Buffett and I don't think I am going to be like him. That is an acknowledgement on my part as to my inclinations towards investing. Perhaps when I have a portfolio worth hundreds of millions of dollars, I might consider trying to assess a company for its competitive advantage. But by and large as I have seen, competitive advantages for most companies tend to erode over time.

So back to what I have mentioned about one of my maiden experiences on investing which was Matex International. It soared some 60% in months. Compared to the rest of my portfolio which consisted of stocks which has competitive advantages laden within them, this company made a positive dent in my portfolio.

What I have figured out over time is that in order for investors to be very successful in investing, one must stand or make bets which are in direct opposition to the crowd. This principle is the principle of contrarianism. Be part of the crowd and one loses. Stand apart from the crowd and one wins. That will be a basic principle that if one embraces, will make for a great investing journey.

In essence, when it comes to investing or rather, deep value investing, invest in the boring, unsexy and unglamorous companies out there. And I think you will do pretty well.

This is part of a series of books which is really an in depth look into my myriad thoughts on value investing and deep value investing, percolating into my consciousness every single day. I was apprehensive at first. Why would I even write a series of books on finance, investing and business? After all, I am not a brand name. I am nobody. My writing of this book really has got nothing to do with trying to gain an audience of any but rather, it is an honest self-expression of my soul's very being.

To all my readers, wherever you may be, may you be blessed with a great prosperity, abundance and happiness!

Why You Should Read This Book

In my mind, the deep value strategy is one that can help the amateur investor outperform the market and perhaps build a rather large portfolio over time. My number is $20 million. And my reasons for stating that will be mentioned throughout this book. For most of us investors, our portfolios are small. And to me, that is an incredible advantage compared to the mutual fund which manages billions of dollars.

Small is good because you can search out unloved, boring companies on the verge of an upswing in stock prices. Small is also great because you can buy companies that are shunned by institutional investors and the crowd.

I have made every attempt to make this topic as simple as possible for the amateur investor. If you want something that is simple to understand and implement, this is it for you.

Also, if eventually, you would like to escape the rat race, reach escape velocity where one's portfolio begins to replace one's earned income, then this is for you as well. These set of strategies are by far the simplest, overlooked, highest compounding investing strategies that I have ever come across.

Without a doubt, I would be a deep value investor for a long time to come.

For investors with some level of experience, what you will get is an honest overview of what deep value investing is and how it can affect your portfolio positively.

Included within the pages of this book are several case studies of companies which can be considered deep value investing candidates.

I think that readers to this book will benefit in the sense that they will immediately get what works and really avoid the pitfalls of investing. After all, no one wants to spend years experimenting and getting on the wrong side of those experiments. This book is for investors who want to avoid making those costly investing mistakes. By reading this book, you will learn to reduce your investment mistakes, prevent loss of money, save your precious time when it comes to investment research and garner good returns as an investor.

Note: All figures reflected in the case studies within this book are correct at the time of publishing. The share prices and figures are also split adjusted where necessary for easy comprehension and comparison.

Table of Contents

Why I Wrote This Book

Why You Should Read This Book

Chapter 1. An Early Start To Investing – Be A Serial Compounder

Chapter 2. Value Investing Through The Eyes Of Buffett And The Media

Chapter 3. To Rely On Expert Predictions Is Futile

Chapter 4. Deep Value Investing -

The Compounding Machine

Chapter 5. Characteristics Of Unloved Stocks

Chapter 6. Institutional Interest In

Net Current Asset Value Stocks

Chapter 7. Graham's Final Interview

Chapter 8. My Maiden Investment Experience – 50% In 6 Months

Resources at

www.theholyfinancier.com

About The Author

Other Books By Kingsley

Chapter 1. An Early Start To Investing – Be A Serial Compounder

In general, the earlier one starts investing the better. Then, one makes use of time as a tool to really get to the point when investing becomes a means to support one's lifestyle and family. And time is very important when it comes to investing. Think about it this way. $1 million, if grown at 15% per annum would result in $150,000 of added income in just 1 year.

If that same million dollars grows at a compounded annual growth rate of 15% per year for 20 years, that would result in an ending portfolio value of approximately $16.4 million. That is an added income of approximately $15.4 million over 20 years.

Well, I believe that you get the idea. Hence, the way to approach investing is to start as young as possible. Now, even if you are in your 30s or 40s, it is really not too late to start. Start investing anyway. Each year of procrastination would mean a potential opportunity cost of your investment return percentage multiplied by your investment amount. Let us then play a game of numbers and possibilities. Let's say you have $1 million dollars and you invested that over 30 years that would result in $66.2 million in ending portfolio value.

As you can see, the longer the runway, the better it is for you in general. The whole idea along the way is to not make those disastrous errors that make for poor investment results.

Perhaps, the example stated above may not be realistic for some of you. How about we start with a beginning amount of just $20,000 and then compound it at 15% per annum over 30 years. That will result in an ending portfolio value of approximately $1.3 million.

Now that is not too shabby isn't it?

Now, what is even better is that periodically, you inject capital into your portfolio. So based on the preceding example, if you inject $20,000 into your portfolio every year, you would get an ending portfolio amount of more than $1.3 million after 30 years.

The sky is practically the limit.

Now to give you an idea of what you can achieve, we really have to look towards one of my heroes. His name is Walter Schloss. Some of you might have heard of him. In the investment world, the man is considered a legend.

From 1956 to 1984, it is understood from several sources that Walter Schloss had a very impressive track record of a compounded annual growth rate of 21.3%. Do you have any idea how brilliant that track record is compared to many hedge fund managers who are actually underperforming the general stock markets? That is nothing short of complete genius in my opinion.

And admittedly, Walter Schloss is one stubborn man. With Warren Buffett deviating from Benjamin Graham's philosophy as he morphed as an investor, here was a man who stuck to what Ben taught him.

Just to give you an idea, $10 000 would become approximately $3.3 million in 30 years. Now the question is can we ordinary mortals do it? The answer is yes we can. In the chapters that continue, I hope to be able to piece together the jigsaw puzzle of investing and to help shed some light on the direction that you should take as an investor. Many of you have accumulated savings in the hundreds of thousands of dollars. That money can be put to good use instead of leaving it lying in the bank. And I am not saying that you can just for the heck of it but deep down, I genuinely believe that with the right mindset and expectations, one can really do tremendously well in investing.

SAVING AS YOU EARN

For starters, as you build your investment portfolio, you will be primarily funding your portfolio through your savings. Therefore, the more you save the better. And as your portfolio results grow, you will see that you would have more confidence to put your savings into your portfolio instead of a legitimate bank account. Bank accounts worldwide pay paltry returns compared to the returns that one can generate in the stock market.

By employing the right set of strategies, one is able to use the stock market as one's bank account instead. That is also the reason why many investors, as they gain confidence in their investing abilities would prefer to invest their money rather than to leave their money in the bank account.

FORCE YOURSELF TO SAVE MONEY

It is thus critical for the reasons mentioned in prior paragraphs that one should make every attempt to save. I am tempted to say that you should save between 20% to 30% of your income. But who am I to judge anyway? You may have your commitments with family and just life. But the old adage "It is not how much you earn but how much you save" does make sense when it comes to investing.

I personally think that targeting to save 20% to 30% of your income is a great start compared to saving nothing at all.

THE RULE OF 72

The rule of 72 is a quick method of estimating the number of years it takes to double your investment. For example, if your portfolio can grow at an approximate 15% per annum, you portfolio will take 4.8 years to double.

That means that your portfolio will double in 4.8 years.

How is 4.8 years arrived at?

One simple does this:

$72 \div 15 = 4.8$

So one's portfolio will double from $1 million to $2 million in 4.8 years.

Now the thing is this. As an investor, you could very well compound your money between 20% to 30% per annum for the first 5 to 10 years. I am going to talk about one such strategy in the later chapters that will help you do just that.

If you are able to compound your money at 20% per annum for 10 years, it would only take you approximately 3.6 years to double your money. That means that, every 3.6 years, the value of your portfolio doubles. $1 in 10 years will become approximately $6.20.

$1 million becomes $6.2 million.

ESCAPE VELOCITY

The idea of escape velocity does not just apply to physics. It also does apply to wealth and our finances. Let me tease you with the idea of escape velocity.

In physics, escape velocity is the minimum speed that an object needs to escape from the gravitational pull of a large object.

When it comes to wealth, financial escape velocity is the minimum income one needs to really live life freely and escape the clutches of the rat race. Let me give you my thoughts on that.

Suppose you say that you need $100 000 annually to get by in any given year, to support your family, to pay the mortgage. We can work backwards from that amount. Let us say that you can compound money at 20% annually. $100 000 ÷ 0.2 = $500 000

You would need at least a portfolio of $500 000 in order to get a $100 000 return.

Now the problem is this though. That $100 000 of return spent means that the portfolio stays at $500 000 perpetually with a 20% return per year. That means, your wealth stays the same even though you are earning $100 000 per year on your portfolio every year as you draw upon that for use in your expenses.

So in your initial years as a serial compounder, make the utmost effort to reduce your expenses and save more. The amount undrawn should be reinvested into the portfolio.

So in the case above, perhaps it may be a good idea to spend $60 000 of the $100 000 in investment return per year and reinvest the rest of the $40 000 into the portfolio.

When the portfolio reaches an amount of $1 million, a 20% return would mean $200 000. So at this point you can safely spend $100 000 and life starts to get more comfortable. In a sense you would have reached your escape velocity.

I would recommend that you get the support of your spouse and family on this matter if you are married. Commitment to this end by two individuals walking this journey of life together would make the goal easier to reach. Remember, the sky is the limit. Perhaps, it is that sea front villa in Bali that you would like to buy some day. Work towards it and make it a part of your reality.

SUMMARY
- Save as much money as you can
- Inject funds into your portfolio periodically once you become adept at investing
- Compound at high rates of return
- Use time as a friend to grow your portfolio
- Be disciplined about investing and saving your money
- Learn to love investing and make it a part of your life

Chapter 2. Value Investing Through the Eyes Of Buffett And The Media

If you would like to know what value investing is in general, it is the art of buying securities at a price less than its intrinsic value. The problem is that the intrinsic value is sometimes very hard to determine in practice. Traditional value investing is just what Warren Buffett expounds so often. Warren claims that value and growth are both joined at the hip.

That means to value a stock, if an investor can make reasonable projections of the future as to the company's revenue, gross profits, earnings, earnings per share or free cash flows, then one can either apply a certain multiple to those earnings based figures and get an intrinsic value. Another way to get the approximate intrinsic value of a company is to discount those free cash flows to the present day to come up with a value of the stock.

And of course, enter the concept of a moated stock or a stock with a competitive advantage so large that it would be virtually impossible for a competitor to actually take away the incumbent's market share.

The term moat is a term popularised by Warren Buffett. It signifies the protective structure around a castle. The metaphor of a moat represents defensibility. Marauding invaders fall into the moat, a ditch, separating the castle from the invaders who attack the castle.

The imagery is vivid. The war cries echo in one's mind. The idea of a moat does seem for all intents and purposes, a great idea through which to explain an investment strategy.

Let me explain further the idea of a moat.

A company that has a moat is able to earn a sustainably high return on equity for very long periods of time. That being the case, the net worth or the book value of the company will tend to grow. The book value is equal to all the assets within a company less all its liabilities.

Now, if one buys a company like that, a price that is below its intrinsic value, then the company would be said to be undervalued.

In general, companies like that tend to have growing earnings, growing cash flows, growing free cash flows and predictable dividend growth. In general, the growth of earnings will cause the company's share price to really march up in tandem. So another principle here is that earnings growth will cause share price to move up in general.

Why is that so?

Whenever there is an announcement of an earnings hike or jump, analysts on Wall Street or in any market around the world would have to revise their estimates of the company upwards. Typically, a new price target will be issued which is much higher than the last traded price.

As an oversimplified example, if a company in a certain industry tends to trade at 15 times earnings and currently has an earnings per share of $2. If the newly announced earnings per share for the latest financial year is $3, the company should trade at $45.

15 x $3 = $45

So previously it may have traded at:

15 x $2 = $30

Hence, generally as earnings grow and exceed analyst expectations, share prices will move upwards.

But what if earnings per share did not grow as predicted? What will happen to the stock price of the company?

Let us take the example of Valeant Pharmaceuticals.

Its diluted earnings per share can be summarised from the table below.

Year	2012	2013	2014	2015	2016
Diluted Earnings Per Share	- $0.38	-$2.70	$2.58	-$0.85	-$6.94

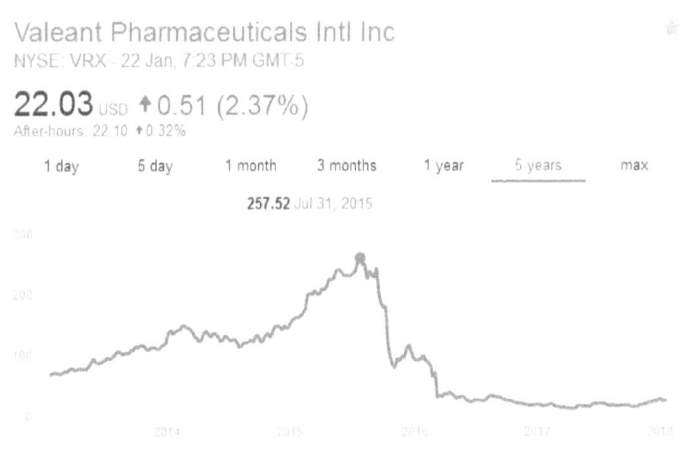

Source: Google

So as you can see 2013 to 2014 were great years with regards to growth. Earnings per share went from negative to $2.58.

But in 2015, as the markets started to sniff out what was wrong with Valeant Pharmaceuticals, the short sellers and other factors caused the stock price to fall drastically over the course of 6 months. There is much more that I can share with regards to Valeant Pharmaceuticals but I will reserve that, possibly for another book.

From 2014 to 2015, earnings per share fell from $2.58 to -$0.85. That caused the stock price to plummet from approximately $260 to $50. A very popular fund manager, Bill Ackman, who was an activist in the company defended the company publicly only to cuts his losses by selling out his position later on. The media coverage around it was a wild frenzy then.

So to answer the question on what will happen when earnings per share figures fall, the share price may fall disproportionately.

Source: Morningstar

And let us take a look at the price to earnings ratio of the company from years 2009 to 2016. Can you see the wild fluctuation?

In 2009, the PE ratio was 12.58 and in 2014, it was 92.93. For the years with a dash, no PE ratio was recorded because earnings were presumably negative.

So within this example alone, if an amateur investor were to bet that earnings will grow, he may be terribly disappointed when that projection does not materialise. When investors are disappointed with earnings growth, there will be a sell down of the stock. The sell down of the stock is especially great when the stock is a well-covered stock in the media and on Wall Street.

And the other thing is that the market's idea of the PE ratio accorded to this company changes very drastically. So perhaps, the earnings may have grown but the market may accord a lower PE ratio than before. This is to be expected in a sentimentally driven market.

Of course there are instances where betting on earnings growth is really rewarding. An example would be Amazon.

Source: Google

Financials		2009	2010	2011	2012	2013	2014	2015	2016
Revenue (Bil)					61.09	74.45	88.99	107.01	135.99
Operating Income (Bil)					0.68	0.75	0.18	2.23	4.19
Operating Margin %					1.11	1.00	0.20	2.09	3.08
Net Income (Bil)					-0.04	0.27	-0.24	0.60	2.37
Diluted Earnings Per Share					-0.09	0.59	-0.52	1.25	4.90

Source: Morningstar

In general, you can see the diluted earnings per share increasing over the last 5 years for Amazon. And the stock price reacts accordingly by going upwards.

So, the central question to ask is this. Is an amateur investor or an investor with some experience, able to focus on the income statement and the cash flow statements of the company and predict, foresee that earnings per share will grow with a high level of certainty? If you are great in this, then it would make sense for you to be a moated investor and look for companies that can grow sustainably.

But in my experience, it is not so simple for many of us, experts included. Many of us get these estimates and predictions wrong.

This was what Ben Graham said of prediction and forecasting in an interview.

"Well, they would claim that if they are correct in their basic contentions about the efficient market, the thing for people to do is to try to study the behaviour of stock prices and try to profit from these interpretations. To me, that is not a very encouraging conclusion because if I have noticed anything over these 60 years on Wall Street, it is that people do not succeed in forecasting what's going to happen to the stock market."

So with Ben Graham's observation of 60 years on Wall Street, he has not seen success with regards to the forecasting of stock prices.

The problem with the human mind is that it has a tendency to attach an arrow to a trend. Usually that trend doesn't last for very long. Hence, predictions may miss the mark entirely very often.

Another example of a company with less drastic fall in earnings is Prophecy International Holdings Ltd.

Financials		2010	2011	2012	2013	2014	2015	2016	2017
Revenue (Mil)		D	D	D	0.66	6.87	9.86	14.03	8.18
Operating Income (Mil)		D	D	D	1.55	1.11	2.96	3.40	-0.63
Operating Margin %		D	D	D	23.26	16.11	30.00	23.21	-6.89
Net Income (Mil)		D	D	D	1.27	0.91	2.33	2.40	1.90
Diluted Earnings Per Share		D	D	D	0.03	0.02	0.04	0.04	0.03

The company's earnings per share was AUD$0.04, AUD$0.04 and AUD$0.03 for 2015, 2016 and 2017 respectively. The stock price dropped from a high of AUD$2.50 to AUD$0.44, which is an extremely drastic drop caused by a 1 cent reduction in earnings per share from 2016 to 2017. Again, buying because you feel that earnings are going to increase is not a great strategy in my opinion unless you reach a level of investing proficiency where you become as skilled as Warren Buffett. And the truth of the matter is few people are as skilled as Warren Buffett.

On the face of it, it sure looks like an overreaction on the markets part but that is how markets work when there is a fixation on earnings. As investors then, our main goal should be to try to take advantage of that overreaction.

So a huge reason as to why investors and fund managers are struggling to compound their portfolio at a rate greater than the markets such as S&P 500 or a relevant index is because of the over fixation on the earnings of companies.

And as investors, the fixation on earnings is what we should avoid, as we begin our journey in investing.

Summary

- The media glamorizes value investing as the Warren Buffett style of investing
- Earning projections are often wrong
- When earnings increase, share prices tend to move upwards

Chapter 3. To Rely On Expert Predictions Is Futile

"The stock market has forecast nine of the last five recessions." - Paul Samuelson

Participants in the stock markets are interested in information on market outlooks, trends and predictions. There seems to be an insatiable demand for such information that every now and then, experts are invited to speak on TV and at conferences. Then, their predictions are aired to humanity.

To the common man on the street, these predictions make all the sense in the world until they realize at some point that these predictions are nothing but fluff. The majority of investors do not even track what had been predicted versus what had occurred in reality. In fact, as these experts often do, their predictions are wrong by a wide margin. In this chapter, I will provide some examples of predictions that were so different from reality to prove my point that predictions of any sort are really an exercise in futility.

A famous economist known as Irving Fisher was lauded as one of the finest economists that the United States has ever produced. However, 9 days before the stock market crashed, he revealed his predictions. He claims then that the "stocks have reached a permanently high plateau."

In another headline published on the New York Times on the 22nd of October 1929, "Fisher Says Prices Of Stocks Are Low." He went on to say that fundamentals were strong and that stock markets were undervalued. 2 days after the New York Times article, the stock market crashed, revealing the foolishness of his statements. He tried to recover from these statements by reframing them positively.

However, this event proved to be a dent to his reputation as the greatest economist the United States has ever produced. By November of 1929, the stock market had declined by more than 30% from its peak. Reportedly, Irving Fisher made those comments after deep research into the data on corporate earnings, capital investments in R&D and valuation of corporate entities as a whole.

The predictions were way off, by such a wide margin that modern day economists and media frequently cite his predictions in 1929 as being terribly optimistic. On hindsight of course, it is easy for us to critique Fisher. However, time and time again throughout the annals of time, most predictions have proven to be more wrong than right.

Another example of a prediction gone wrong is the prediction of online shopping. In around 1966, Time Magazine projected time forward to the year 2000 and made a seriously inaccurate prediction which is now cited as one of the worst predictions of all time. Time Magazine wrote "Remote shopping while entirely feasible will flop."

They further substantiated that statement by saying that women as a whole would prefer getting out there to buy things physically. All of us living in this day and age know how wrong that prediction went. Today, we see ecommerce giants such as Amazon and Alibaba doing a net annual sales of $156 billion and $23 billion respectively. Along the way as well, many experts made predictions about Amazon that left one puzzled considering what has happened to this very day. And all of these predictions are forgotten in the annals of time.

In 2016, Amazon reported approximately $2.3 billion in net profit to its common stockholders. In 2017's Black Friday alone, there were 7.14 million transactions which took place on Amazon's platform. This was more than the combined transactions on Walmart, Kohl's and Target. In fact even if we added up all the transactions that occurred at Walmart, Best Buy, Kohl's, Target, Macy's. Home Depot and Toys "R" Us, we will find that the combined transactions that happened over these retailers would pale in comparison to the mighty Amazon. Again, the prediction about online shopping decades earlier proved to be entirely inaccurate.

Last but not least, Bloomberg ran an article "Prediction: Apple Predictions Will Be Wrong Again". It is once again the season for financial predictions gone wrong as the author points out. Before a new IPhone model launches some 14 months out, analysts are busying themselves studying factory output, doing surveys that help to ascertain the quantity of new batches of IPhone being produced. Combined with sales forecasts, they try to arrive at an estimated prediction of Apple's sales revenue. From the estimated sales revenue, net income figures are extrapolated. From those net income figures, an analyst can set renewed price targets for Apple Inc.

The thing is that historically, these predictions have often been so wrong that it shows us how pointless these predictions and all this work of forecasting really is.

In July 2014, the analyst consensus was $195 billion in sales revenue for the fiscal year ending in September 2015. In 2015 however, Apple reported $234 billion in sales revenue. In July 2015, analysts predicted a projected sales revenue of $246 billion for the fiscal year ending in

September 2016. Actual figures reported by Apple was $216 billion.

All in all, the projected sales revenue by these analysts were either underestimated by 12% or overestimated by 20% over the last 2 years. Of course these are not the only instances that show that analysts' estimates miss the mark all too often when making predictions. In David Dreman's "Bubbles and the Role of Analyst's Forecast.", it was stated that analysts had a role in making securities look cheaper than it really was and more often than not, their predictions were off by a wide margin.

So the question then is why even bother to rely on predictions of any sort when we all know that time after time, many of these expert predictions are wrong. The idea then, when it comes to investing is to stick to the numbers. A company is only undervalued if the analysis of the balance sheets, income statements and cash flow statements tell you so.

Typically, in my experience, what I see is this. Analysts orchestrate action on a company by issuing buy calls and upgrade a stock. Stock market participants respond to these calls by pushing the prices of these stocks up. Now, very often, when I look at some of these companies that are upgraded through the eyes of a deep value investor, I wouldn't even bother with many of them because at this point, the markets have acknowledged the stock's value. Very often, when I start buying, there is no analyst research coming onto the scene for the particular company that I purchased.

Contrarianism is a lonely journey but it is rewarding. And when a positive research report comes out on the company that I bought into that was previously beaten down, it is time to start thinking about selling. Do track some of these reports because some of these analysts have got great insights into these companies. But nonetheless, their predictions are so far off that to pay any heed to them would mean that one would not capture as much profits as when one bought it at a totally unloved price.

Sometimes a company turns out to have some growth. This is the hard part of it all - deciding when to sell. What I would like to do is to have an understanding that there may be some growth of earnings 1 to 2 years down the road. If and when that happens, it is not hard to see that an investment like that may turn into a multi-bagger investment. And as an investor, I will sell into those rising prices. There are a myriad ways to look into the decision of selling. But for now, I leave you with this. Don't even bother relying on an analyst report. If you do, you will be part of the crowd that experiences mediocre returns. Here, I leave you with yet another quote to ponder on.

"We have long felt that the only value of stock forecasters is to make fortune tellers look good." - Warren Buffett

Chapter 4. Deep Value Investing - The Compounding Machine

The terms deep value investing lends itself to scrutiny by value investors because I do not believe that these terms were invented by Ben Graham himself. Rather these terms were popularised by modern day practitioners of Ben Graham's value strategies.

Unlike Warren Buffett, Ben Graham would never put himself in the position to buy a moated company if the price was not cheap enough. While Warren Buffett looks for companies with a sustainable competitive advantage and buy these companies at a fair price, Graham prefers to go by the numbers. By that, I mean that Graham looks for obvious bargains. His preference is a cheapness validated by statistics. He wants to go strictly by the numbers.

My interpretation of the matter is this. While Buffett tries to value the company against the company's purchase price at a point in time, Graham does not try to value the company. Instead, he tries to find a floor for what prices might potentially trade at and buys near that floor. These group of companies are so cheap that they are considered statistical bargains by the investment community. As long as these companies are statistically cheap, Graham will buy them. Notably, he does not focus very heavily on factors such as the quality of management and concern himself too much with projected earnings.

But oftentimes, these companies have problems that the investment community does not look upon favourably. And that in itself is a predictor of one's success ironically. In order for a investors to make money easily in stocks, they have to buy the unwanted, discarded and unloved stocks by the investment community.

There are several approaches and themes to buying deeply discounted securities. In general, a deep value approach is really a strategy that focuses on a low price in relation to the assets that a company has on the balance sheet and its earnings.

The approach that we are going to focus on today is the net current asset value approach because in our opinion, it is simple to use and can be used to compound money at very high rates of return for a long time. The only limitation is that once your portfolio's size reach approximately $20 million, you will find some difficulty in fully deploying your capital.

The reason for the statement above is because such companies are few and far between. They are very scarce indeed. But of the entire universe of stocks, one will find that these stocks are amongst the cheapest stocks that one will ever find.

Net Current Asset Value & The Liquidation Value

During the years of the great depression, Graham found that many companies were trading below the approximate liquidation value. If these companies were to be liquidated, stockholders will get more than was paid at those sub-liquidation prices. This approximate liquidation value, can be derived from the balance sheet and estimated in a very conservative way. Henceforth, the net current asset value approach was born. An approach so simple and somewhat arcane that investors simply do not appreciate its profound simplicity in building wealth.

On the balance sheet, we can find figures such as the current assets, non-current assets, current liabilities and non-current liabilities. The balance sheet is a snapshot of the company's financial health at a given point in time, that is, on a certain date.

Graham proposed that if one were to take the most liquid assets and subtract all liabilities and preferred stock while ignoring any value on non-current assets, that resultant value will be a very conservative liquidation value of the company. That is, if all of the company's current assets were sold and the proceeds were used to pay off all liabilities on the balance sheet, that residual value would be what is paid to common stockholders.

That residual value is called the liquidation value and this value presupposes if the company is shut down, all remaining proceeds or residual value is given back to shareholders. Very often, these companies will not go through a formal liquidation process because it is not as easy to liquidate a company now compared to Graham's time.

The idea however is that if a company were to be considered a going concern in a sense that it is profitable and will be profitable in the future, how would it make sense that the company is trading at a price below liquidation value? If must be worth more than its liquidation value for every single year of profitability strengthens the balance sheet, increases the liquidation value, and on top of that, for the cream of the crop for these group of companies, they represent undervalued and potential takeover targets although it is not necessary that a takeover of the company occurs.

An example here would suffice. If you do not mind, I love the idea of teaching by using examples. There is no compulsion to believe every single word I say. Read, ponder and discover through your very effort that this is something that is worthwhile pursuing.

Source: Google

There is a company called Charle Co Ltd, listed in the Tokyo stock exchange. We purchased it at a price of ¥500. At that time, the company had an approximate liquidation value or net current asset value per share of ¥1000. It was trading at a 50% discount to its estimated liquidation value, estimated via its net current asset value per share calculation. And I am going to quote its net income from 2013 to 2017. The net income figures are ¥0.42 billion, ¥0.4 billion, ¥1.01 billion, ¥1 billion, and ¥0.28 billion for 2013 till 2017 respectively.

Now the question is this then. How is it possible that a company that is operating profitably year after year for the past 5 years trade under its liquidation value? Well, to answer that, the market is simply too earnings obsessed to look at the balance sheet of some of these companies. Earnings are hard to forecast and if you are going to play that game, you'd better be really good at it.

Now if you look at the years 2016 and 2017, you will see that the net income tapered off in a big way from ¥1 billion to ¥0.28 billion. In 2016, Charle Co in fact traded mostly at less than ¥500, at around ¥460. Why didn't the price drop further? Well, for one, the company was already trading below its liquidation value. That liquidation value provided a floor so to speak. In fact, it is my experience, when companies are trading below liquidation value, there is such a dearth of institutional interest that these companies trade at pennies on the dollar.

If you are interested in deep value, net current asset value stocks from Japan, I have written numerous case studies of Japanese stocks which have yielded in excess of 100% returns. The book is called: *The $20 Million Investor Blueprint: Deep Value Net Current Asset Value Stocks In Japan.* And indeed, the net current asset value strategy does work in Japan as well.

Let us compare the performance of Charle Co to Domino's Pizza Enterprises Limited.

Source: Google

The net income was $28.66 million, $42.3 million, $64.05 million, $82.43 million, and $102.86 million from 2013 to 2017 respectively. Now, you do notice earnings trending upwards but look at the charts of Domino's and you will see the price trading down from $72 to $47. The price to book ratio is incidentally 9.87 at the time of this writing, a very high price in relation to its assets.

The 2 examples given above are meant to change your paradigm of thinking when it comes to investing. All of our books by TheHolyFinancier will be peppered with examples so as to make you re-anchor and rewire your brain for investment success. It is your destiny to be able to purchase this book. Make it your destiny to be prosperous then!

Now, let us look at one of Warren Buffett's recent buys. IBM.

Source: Google

It is understood that Berkshire's average purchase price was about $170. Buffett, through Berkshire Hathaway, accumulated a large stake of 8.6% over the years but it has not done very much for him.

I can't for the life of me see why he actually purchased IBM. But we have to understand that Buffett is an elephant in the investment world. The size of his portfolio will not allow him to purchase a small or midcap. It is just not an efficient way to deploy capital.

Anecdotally, deep value investing does work based on my experience compared to other strategies. And furthermore, your size is your advantage for now. Till the portfolio reaches a size of tens of millions of dollars, which incidentally is a great problem to have, many investors will do very well with the net current asset value strategy. In my opinion, the deep value strategy theme of using the net current asset value is able to compound money at the highest rates of return.

Graham's Record

From 1936 to 1956, Ben Graham compounded money, through his investment firm, at a compounded annual growth rate of 20%. The markets on the other hand did 12.2% of annualised return over the same time span. If you would compound your money like how Ben did for a long period of time, there is absolutely no reason that you cannot reach your financial goals.

Scarcity Of Such Stocks

In the entire universe of stocks in USA of approximate 4000 NYSE and NASDAQ stocks and a further 8000 - 10000 stocks which are traded over the counter, according to my research and screeners as I write this chapter, I can only find about 10 such stocks which trade well below the liquidation value of the company.

In the first place, it is very difficult to find a company whose current assets exceed its total liabilities. It is abnormal to find operating companies which have an enormous current asset base and a small total liability base.

And the other thing with regards to conservatism is this. The entire value of non-current assets which include plant, property and equipment is entirely disregarded by Graham. Such assets do have value. Land has value. Property has value. However, Graham disregards this as he calculates the liquidation value of the company.

This speaks of the tremendous conservatism of Ben Graham as an investor.

Formula To Calculate Net Current Asset Value

The net current asset value can be calculated by the formula given below:

Current assets - Total Liabilities - Preferred Stock

Now preferred stock is a class of ownership in a company that has a higher claim on assets and earnings before common stock. As an investor buying common stock which is publicly traded on an exchange, the formula above treats preferred stock as a form of debt which ranks higher than common stock. In fact, preferred stock is a hybrid asset that has characteristics of both equity and debt.

The treatment of subtracting preferred stock from current assets is indeed conservative and appropriate because a dividend must be paid out to preferred stockholders even before common stockholders are paid. Apart from that, depending on how some issues are structured, preferred stockholders are entitled to dividends in arrears. That is, if dividends have been suspended by a company for a period of time, preferred stockholders are entitled to claw back those unpaid dividends when the company can pay them.

In cases of financial distress of a company, creditors and preferred stockholders are paid off first. The remnant residual value is paid off to common stockholders.

In any case, common stockholders and preferred stockholders are subordinate to bondholders or creditors. That means that bondholders must be paid first. Then preferred stockholders are paid. And lastly common stockholders are paid.

The next formula that one must know is this:

$$\text{Net Current Asset Value Per Share} = \text{Net Current Asset Value} \div \text{Total Number Of Shares Outstanding}$$

What we have now is the net current asset value per share. Generally speaking, we would like to see net current value per share growing over time. This means that the company is profitable and its current assets are growing and/or its total liabilities are decreasing. This is a good thing.

Next, once the net current asset value per share is calculated, compare the price per share of the company to the net current asset value per share. If the price per share is two-thirds or less than the net current asset value per share, this company can be put under consideration for a purchase.

Summary

- Deep value strategy can compound money at high rates of return
- The net current asset value theme is a great theme to start from
- Buying the cheapest of the cheapest stocks does make a difference to long term results

Chapter 5. Characteristics Of Unloved Stocks

When it comes to deep value investing, one has to be comfortable with some of these stocks which pass the deep value criteria. Typically, these stocks trade at a low price to book value. Now, because I only buy the cheapest of the cheapest stocks, I would only buy a company if the company is trading at 2-thirds or less than the liquidation value.

While book value is a measure of net worth, book value still records the value of intangibles whose value can disappear overnight due to write downs. A better estimate for the net worth of a company is the net tangible book value. An even more conservative measure of net worth is the liquidation value which is the net current asset value. The net current asset value is the estimated liquidation value if all of its assets were liquidated and all of the company's liabilities were to be paid off.

Now, for most investors, buying some of these tremendously undervalued stocks will take some getting used to. There are many reasons as to why these companies are trading at such low prices. For most investors who want to be deep value investors, the brain must be reprogrammed from "buying wonderful companies at a fair price" to "buying really cheap companies, taking care of the downside first and then worrying about the upside later".

The idea is simply survival first taking precedence to profits. Here are my thought processes. If I can get these companies at such low prices and if these companies can survive the next few years, chances are that its stock prices will revert to a mean. Even better, if the company can thrive in some way over the next few years, we could hold on for a good profit. So, the idea really is one of survival first, then profits second.

There are many reasons why a company is available at such cheap prices. The first reason that comes to me from my experience is that the industry may be doing very badly. As a result, the stock prices tank and cause some of these companies to trade at a price less than its book value. Even better, some of these which happen to be the cheapest of the cheapest, trade at prices less than 2-thirds of its liquidation value.

An example of such a company is Thalassa Holdings. It is a company that specialises in supplying robotics solutions, equipment and services for the energy and marine companies that conduct exploration and production of oil. In 2014, oil prices started to tank. Companies in the oil and gas industry started to reduce capital expenditures as most were in the red. This evidently affected Thalassa Holdings when its revenue per share dropped from £1.14 in 2013 to £0.40 and £0.51 in 2014 and 2015 respectively.

Source: Google

As a result, loss per share became -£0.31 and -£0.33 respectively in 2014 and 2015. The price of Thalassa Holdings was £0.34 in January 2016. The net current asset value per share as reflected in the FY 2015 annual report was approximately £0.46.

Today, at the time of this writing, the share price is £0.92. Many a time, the best time to buy is when the company is losing money. And when the industry and earnings recover, prices tend to move up. I have personally experienced incidents where the company's earnings did not recover. However, negative sentiments around the company subsided and the share price rose subsequently. This may not sound intuitive but that is what mean reversion is all about. Extremes in prices tend to revert to a mean.

There are a whole lot of negative circumstances surrounding Thalassa Holdings then. However, at that time, it had an activist, Duncan Soukup at the helm. That is often a good sign. At least, someone bothers enough to try to charter the company out of troubled waters.

This is an example where buying a loss making company can really add to your wealth. Of course, the next question is when would the company make money again? The truth is you can only estimate when that will take place but more likely than not, that estimate would be wrong. Hence, do not take on a concentrated position with regards to such companies. We can be wrong sometimes.

There are also other reasons why a company may be unloved. The company may have reduced dividends for some reason as in the case of Advanced Holdings.

Advanced Holdings was trading at SGD$0.27 on the Singapore Stock Exchange when we first saw it. In 2014, the dividends paid out were SGD$1.82 million. In 2015 however, it only paid out SGD$0.91 million in dividends. Naturally, its stock price tanked. I am not saying that that is the only reason why the stock price tanked but I would say that it was one of the reasons that caused the stock price to tank. Also, it was affected by the oil and gas industry which was hit by low oil prices. However, months later, it traded at a price of $0.35.

Source: Google

The stock price has not done very much for Advanced Holdings. In fact, it has dropped back down to under $0.30. If anything at all, know that not all your picks will trend up after you buy them. That is to be expected with the net current asset value strategy.

Sometimes a stock is unloved because of its size and management quality. In this case which I encountered, the company was so small that institutional shareholders would not have been able to invest in it. Also, it did not give any dividends for the past 5 years. It was a Canadian company called Imperial Ginseng and at that time it had a market capitalisation of C$4.9 million. The net cash on its balance sheet was C$3.32 million. Also, the company was profitable recording C$1.33 million of net income in 2016.

On the 21st of October 2016 as I researched into Imperial Ginseng, the company was trading at a price of C$0.68. Shortly thereafter, it dropped to C$0.52. Today, the price is C$1.60, approximately 135% of profit if an investor were to have bought it at a price of C$0.68. (If you are interested in more in depth versions of these case studies, do refer to some of the other books I have listed at the end of this book.)

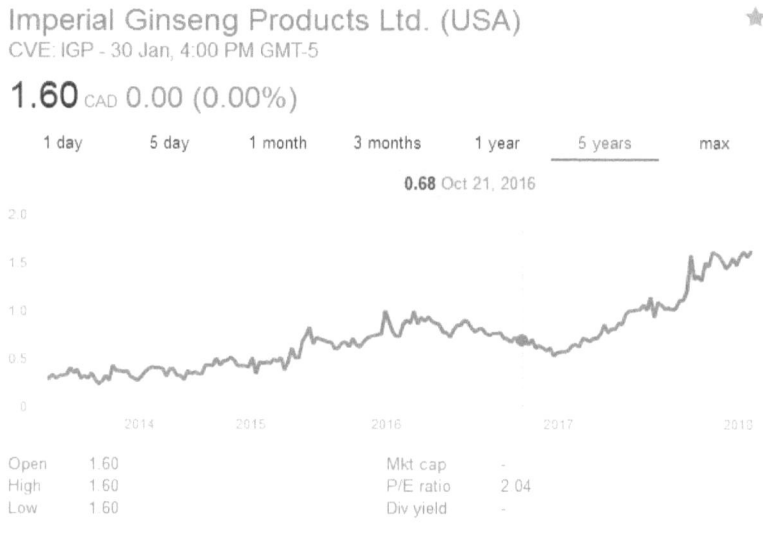

Source: Google

So here we have a company that was small, cheap and unloved. But the company did well from a stock price's perspective.

As you can see, these are companies with a myriad problems. If you'd like to pick on such companies, you would spend all day picking on them till the cows come home. But if you were to look at it from Ben Graham's perspective, you may pounce upon it with gleeful eyes. Below is a short list that explains why some companies are unloved. This list is not meant to be exhaustive.

In summary, characteristics of unloved stocks include:
- Over-indebtedness
- Falling revenues
- Sunset industry
- High interest expenses relative to operating income
- Loss making
- Lack of a dividend policy
- Little to no growth in earnings
- Poor management ability
- Small capitalisation

Chapter 6. Institutional Interest In Net Current Asset Value Stocks

It is my observation that the low levels of institutional ownership corresponds with beaten down, unloved net current asset value stocks and low price to book value stocks. This is something that I have seen over and over again. Institutional ownership is the ownership of shares in a public listed corporation by fund managers and large financial organisations.

In my view, low levels of institutional ownership is one of the reasons that explains why some stocks are so undervalued. We will look at some of these companies, their respective charts and the levels of institutional ownership. The information given here is only reflective of institutional levels of ownership in the company at the time of this writing. Do note that levels of institutional ownership change from time to time.

Wal-Mart Stores Inc

Wal-Mart Stores Inc is perhaps one of the largest and most successful retailers of our generation. It has 3 main business segments. They are Walmart International, Walmart U.S. and Sam's club. They operate on a wholesale basis and a retail basis. Altogether, Walmart is reported to have over 11700 retail stores and approximately $500 billion in annual sales revenue. Walmart's market capitalisation at the time of this writing is $324 billion.

Source: Google

If you have held Walmart for 5 years as an investor, the company really has not done very much for you. At the time of this writing, the stock price is approximately $110, with a surge that occurred over the past 6 months.

Ruane Cunniff, a famous fund manager in around October 2016 had this to say regarding Walmart

"We reduced our holding in Walmart (NYSE:WMT) during the quarter, and exited the stock in early October. Over our 11-year holding period, Walmart generated a positive total shareholder return but modestly underperformed the S&P 500 Index. Walmart remains a formidable company, but over the past decade its dominance has waned.

International expansion has never generated good returns for shareholders, while Walmart has struggled to develop a winning e-commerce strategy. We think higher wages for its entry level workers, continued growth at Amazon and the need to invest heavily in e-commerce will put pressure on Walmart's earnings over the next few years."

Its current price to book ratio is 4.22 and the lowest its price to book value has been is 2.47 in the last 5 years. In January 2005, around the time when Ruane Cunif added Walmart to its portfolio, the price to book ratio of the company was around 4.5.

In January 2004, the price to book ratio was 5.32. Needless to say, Walmart, a company usually earning a return on equity in excess of 20% for the last 5 years suffered a shock when in 2016 and 2017, its reported return on equity was 18.15% and 17.23%. One of the reasons in my mind is the rise of ecommerce giant, Amazon Inc. Once competition sets in, the return on equity for some of these companies will inevitably decline. This is to be expected.

Of course, when Ruane Cunif bought into Walmart some 11 to 12 years back, he believed to have paid a fair price for a wonderful company. Moats and competitive advantages do erode over time especially in the face of a cheaper, more efficient competitor.

Now, with regards to levels of institutional interest, 32.7% of Walmart's stock is owned by institutions.

Amazon.com Inc

Amazon.com is an online retailer with a global presence. It sells products through its marketplace, Amazon.com. It is considered to be one of the largest retailers with a net sales of $136 billion in 2016. On an earnings basis, Amazon trades at a price to earnings of 357. On a price to book basis, it currently trades at about 27 times book value. At the time of this writing, Amazon had a market capitalisation of $683 billion.

Source: Google

Amazon's stock price has multiplied more than 5 fold for the last 5 years. One of the reasons being, it is a very popular stock among fund managers. It is my opinion that Amazon is building a competitive moat that will last years into the future and Jeff Bezos is doing a great job building a customer centric platform. What I fail to see is how long that moat will last. I would not buy it at this price for it is way out of my comfort zone. With regards to levels of institutional interest, institutional ownership stands at 61%.

With such high levels of institutional ownership as I have seen many times, all it takes for a stock to plummet in price is a slight disappointment on the earnings front and there will be a market sell off. Since there are so many institutional investors, a large number of them will try to sell out their stakes at ever decreasing prices. This is one of the reasons I avoid stocks with high levels of institutional ownership. My experience in such stocks have been lacklustre.

Amira Nature Food Ltd

Amira Nature Foods Ltd is a company in India that produces its own Basmati rice and sells them under several brand names worldwide. It is also sells edible oils, snacks and ready to eat meals.

Source: Google

It's all time high over the last 5 years was in 2014 at a price of $22.71. Evidently, it has been heavily beaten down for a number of reasons which I will not go into here. Currently, it is trading at a price of about 55% of the net current asset value or liquidation value. Its price to book value is currently 0.5. Mostly, companies trading at two-thirds or less than the estimated liquidation value, as estimated by the net current asset value formula, also are trading at a low price relative to its book value.

With regards to the levels of institutional ownership in Amira Nature Foods, it stands at 25%. Amira's level of institutional ownership is less than that of Walmart. It's institutional ownership is also less than that of Amazon's.

I believe that Ben Graham would have included this stock into his portfolio.

Gigamedia Ltd

Gigamedia is a company headquartered in Taiwan. It is a publisher of online games in Taiwan, Hong Kong and Macau. It is also a cloud services provider.

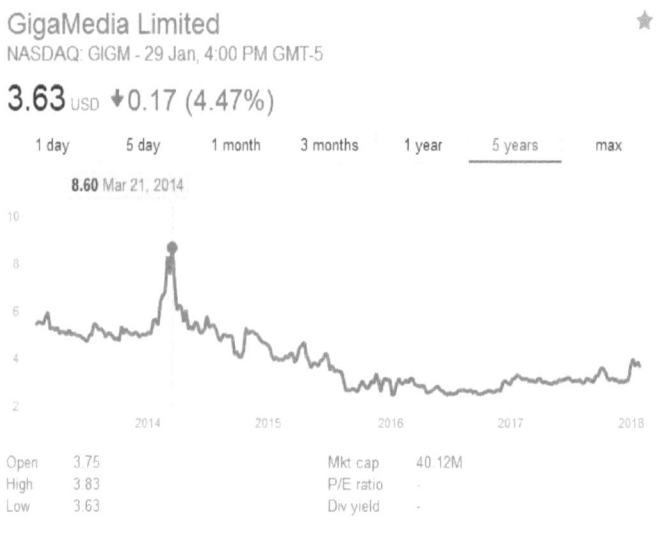

Source: Google

It's all time high over the last 5 years was $8.60. It is currently trading at a price of $3.63 which is approximately 68% of its liquidation value. The price to book ratio for Gigamedia stands at 0.7. Like Amira Nature Foods, the price has been falling for 5 years. Institutional ownership stands at 2.92%. The institutional ownership in this company is very low as compared to many large cap stocks out there.

STR Holdings

STR Holdings is a developer and manufacturer of encapsulants which protect embedded semiconductor circuits of solar panels. It is currently trading at a price of $0.28 and has a market capitalisation of $5.47 million. Its price to book ratio is 0.19 at the time of this writing. The company has struggled for years with losses mounting.

However, quite recently, 51% of the company was bought out by China based, Zhenfa New Energy. More importantly, STR Holdings has no debt. That suggests to me that the company can survive and not go bankrupt over the next few years.

Source: Google

With regards to its level of institutional ownership, that figure stands at 6.7%. Relative to companies with larger market capitalisations, there are low levels of institutional ownership in such unloved companies. STR Holdings is also trading at about 38% of liquidation value at the time of this writing.

If these companies with small levels of institutional ownership manage to stir up investor interest in their stocks, institutional ownership levels will rise and when that happens, stock prices of such companies tend to go up in my experience. On the other hand, when companies which have high levels of institutional ownership disappoint in some small way, the selloff will be drastic.

Hence, using the net current asset value ensures that one stays away from the crowd so to speak. As you can see by now, when one buys into net current asset value stocks, he typically buys when there are low levels of institutional interest. In research done by Navin Chopra, Josef Lakonishok and Jay R. Ritter entitled "Measuring Abnormal Performance", it is found that extreme prior losers outperform extreme prior winners by 5% to 10% per year during the next 5 years. That simply means that stocks which have done poorly over the last 5 years tend to do well over the next 5 years.

Because most investors have a tendency towards herd behaviour, I make the argument through these examples that buying companies trading at less than 2-thirds of liquidation value forces one to stay away from the herd, that is, the institutional investors. And by doing so, an investor can expect investment results which are better than that of the markets.

Chapter 7. Graham's Final Interview

Ben Graham led a purposeful life. For one, he had invented an entire field of security analysis. The other was that he had created a path that many retail investors could tread on. For me, it was a logical approach to hang my hat on. In Ben's final interview, he provided a few nuggets of wisdom and also showed his deep conviction regarding the deep value approach. The first deep value approach that he favoured was the net-net or net working capital approach. The second was buying stocks at less than or equal to a trailing price to earnings multiple of 7.

This was what he had to say regarding the net current asset value approach in his last interview in 1976.

"My first, more limited, technique confines itself to the purchase of common stocks at less than their working-capital value, or net-current-asset value, giving no weight to the plant and other fixed assets, and deducting all liabilities in full from the current assets. We used this approach extensively in managing investment funds, and over a 30-odd year period we must have earned an average of some 20 per cent per year from this source.

For a while, however, after the mid-1950's, this brand of buying opportunity became very scarce because of the pervasive bull market. But it has returned in quantity since the 1973-74 decline. In January 1976 we counted over 300 such issues in the Standard & Poor's Stock Guide--about 10 per cent of the total. I consider it a foolproof method of systematic investment--once again, not on the basis of individual results but in terms of the expectable group outcome."

On the basis of selecting stocks trading at less than two-thirds of the liquidation value, Graham managed to gain an average of 20% per year for over 30 years. This means that a dollar invested will become approximately $237. That is an outstanding track record by any means. Also, one has to understand that Graham was investing primarily in the US then. He acknowledged that sometimes, these opportunities can dry up.

However, because it is easier for us investors to invest beyond our home markets these days, we really have no excuse to make to disregard this simple, profound and highly effective strategy. (I have written a book called: *The $20 Million Investor Blueprint: Net Current Asset Value Strategies For The International Investor* if this is a strategy that you would want to pursue as an investor. I also have 2 other books called *The $20 Million Investor Blueprint: Deep Value Net Current Asset Value Stocks In Japan* and *The $20 Million Investor Blueprint: Net Current Asset Value Stocks In The USA.*)

At this point, I want to stress that while the method is simple and profound, yet, it is difficult to implement. My experiences interlaced with the knowledge that I possess have told me in no uncertain terms that at times, there are instances of you underperforming the markets. In other instances, new fads cause you to have the fear of missing out.

A classic example is the dot-com bubble in 2002 to 2003. Suddenly, you find your friends making more money than you in these markets. The reason is because there is a rush of money into those markets, causing prices to skyrocket. There will be a deprival super reaction on your part as described by Charlie Munger in the Psychology of Human Misjudgement. But the idea is to remain disciplined and stick to your guns when everybody else acts otherwise.

As long are you are focused on implementing the net current asset value strategy, research has shown time and time again that your portfolio will prevail over the market. And over time, if you do that enough, you will become wealthy beyond your imagination.

Chapter 8. My Maiden Investment Experience – 50% In 6 Months

I am inspired to share one of the most profound investing experiences I have ever had. I describe it as losing my investing virginity. Till this day, as I recount these memories with glee in my heart, waves of dopamine flood my body. The experience was profound to me because I was still new to investing then. And of course, the investment resulted in a surprising profit.

To this day, I am grateful for that experience for it etched in my heart that investing need not be as difficult as rocket science. At the same time of course, this is one of those experiences which I will carry with me for the rest of my life. Without this lucky break, I would say that I may not have been the investor I am today. Or at least, I don't think I would have as great a result as I currently have.

The universe and divine providence has been good to me and I hope to pay that forward in some way and spread investing in a manner that helps to light the path of investing. Even in a small way, I would consider that mission somewhat accomplished.

The year was 2007 and I remember I was this wide eyed college kid, eager to learn, trying to assimilate everything that I can from the books I read, from the countless conversations with my finance professors and the frequent exercises of valuing a company. I can honestly say that I knew not a thing then. But the thing about investing is that it is cumulative. Experience has its way of teaching you. Sometimes, you get it. Sometimes you don't. But it all adds up. It took me a while to get this one so I am relaying my experience of this to you.

Matex International was established in 1989 and then listed on the mainboard of the Singapore Exchange in 2004. The company is a manufacturer, supplier and agent of quality dyestuffs, chemicals, colour measurement and computer aided systems to the textile industry. Admittedly, I would call this company a boring one.

Balance Sheets ($'000)			
Fixed Assets	24,828	16,383	17,080
Other non-current assets	2,614	2,736	1,111
Current assets	63,357	62,759	49,613
Less current liabilities	(26,855)	(21,667)	(21,560)
Net current assets	36,502	41,092	28,053
Non-current liabilities	(156)	(1,303)	(74)
	63,788	58,908	46,170
Shareholders' equity	45,059	42,726	30,924
Minority interests	18,729	16,182	15,246
	63,788	58,908	46,170
Net assets value per share (cents)**	25.31	24.00	23.25

Source: 2005 Matex International Annual Report

The net current asset value or the approximate liquidation value can be calculated as:

$$63.357 - 26.855 - 0.156 = 36.346$$

The net current asset value per share was thus 36.346 million by the time the 2005 annual report was published. And at the same time, operating cash flows was positive from 2002 to 2006. Operating cash flow figures came in at $6.63 million, $5.07 million, $6.39 million, $4.33 million, and $1.31 million from 2002 to 2006.

Since there were 178 million shares outstanding, the net current asset value per share can be calculated as:

$$\$36.346 \div 178 \approx \$0.20$$

	FY 2005 Actual	FY 2004 Actual	FY 2003 Actual
Profit and Loss Accounts ($'000)			
Revenue	53,592	50,235	54,765
Profit from operations	5,081	6,536	7,130
Financial expenses	(281)	(80)	(60)
Financial income	328	111	172
	5,128	6,567	7,242
Share of results of associated company	-	-	137
Profit before tax	5,128	6,567	7,379
Income tax	(1,244)	(1,579)	(1,715)
Profit after tax	3,884	4,988	5,664
Minority interests	2,197	2,753	2,733
Net profit attributable to shareholders	1,687	2,235	2,931
	3,884	4,988	5,664
Earnings per share (cents)*	0.95	1.30	2.89

Source: 2005 Matex International Annual Report

Balance Sheets ($'000)			
Property, plant and equipment	26,834	24,828	16,383
Other non-current assets	2,323	2,614	2,736
Current assets	59,090	63,357	62,759
Less current liabilities	(25,318)	(26,855)	(21,667)
Net current assets	33,772	36,502	41,092
Non current liabilities	(100)	(156)	(1,303)
	62,829	63,788	58,908
Shareholders' equity	44,078	45,059	42,726
Minority interests	18,751	18,729	16,182
	62,829	63,788	58,908

Source: Matex International 2006 Annual Report

In 2006, the net current asset value can be calculated as:

$$59.09 - 25.318 - 0.1 = 33.672$$

The net current asset value considering that there were 178 million shares outstanding was:

$$\$33.672 \div 178 \approx \$0.19$$

So the net current asset value per share was between 19 cents to 20 cents.

In around December 2006, the company had reached a new low of 9 cents. At 12 cents, we decided to purchase some shares in Matex International. In a matter of just 6 months, the price rose to 20 cents. Lady luck smiled on me as we managed to sell out at between 18 cents to 20 cents.

The percentage profit was between 50% at 18 cents and 67% at 20 cents and if I were to annualise those figures, that percentage would jump. All in all, a great experience for a student who was trying his hand at investing.

Now, the thing was this. It took me all of 30 minutes to research Matex International. There was no deep dive into its financials. It was a boring company by any measure. In fact, in 2006, there was a loss of 0.12 cents per share. In

2004 and 2005, earnings per share were 1.3 cents and 0.95 cents per share. But nonetheless, the company was trading at a price close to 60% of the liquidation value. It was a company that did not deserve to trade at that price despite earnings per share falling over 3 years in my opinion then as it was mostly profitable.

Now another thing was that I had no real insights. I was not sure what the catalyst was. I was not sure if they were going to hike dividends. I was not sure whether the company was well managed. I was not even sure if the investment would have made any money back then. It was a wild experiment on my part.

I remember at the time, I was also looking into buying wonderful companies at a fair price. The idea was to buy companies with strong competitive advantages and let time be the friend of a wonderful business. Somewhat of an amateur then, I looked towards my hero, Warren Buffett for investment advice. I can't recall the exact time when I bought ConocoPhillips, a company that explores and produces crude oil and natural gas. And one of the reasons why I purchased this company was because Warren Buffett did as well. I tried my best to value the company.

It is funny how when the world's greatest investor buys a company, my biases set in as I look for validation. The fact of the matter was that I did not dare to admit to myself that I did not know enough about the company after weeks of research into it. If you have been a student of corporate finance and "The Theory of Investment Value" by John Burr Williams, you will understand that tweaks to your discount rate could distort the valuation exercise of a company.

Therein lies a lesson of investing. Do not buy stocks just because your favourite investor bought them. Also, one has to be honest with oneself. One has to know thyself. One has to study one's quirks, idiosyncrasies and biases. When it comes to investing, the investor's chief enemy is likely to be himself. I knew then that great investment results do not necessarily correlate with strenuous effort. Also, I found out the hard way that the moated investing game was clearly not for me. Like I said earlier, life has a way of teaching you.

This was what Warren Buffett said about the ConocoPhillips purchase.

"Without urging from Charlie or anyone else, I bought a large amount of ConocoPhillips stock when oil and gas prices were near their peak. I in no way anticipated the dramatic fall in energy prices that occurred in the last half of the year."

Well, Warren Buffett made a very large purchase of ConocoPhillips. He regretted it. The price of oil fell thereafter. Another lesson here perhaps. Don't invest solely on the assumption that a commodity's price will stay constant or increase.

Source: Google

Just after Buffett bought into ConocoPhillips, the company's price tanked. It fell to around a low of $29 before recovering to the same level some 4 to 5 years later. Just imagine for a moment here. How much time did I waste trying to be like Warren Buffett, reading all those books written on him by eager authors cashing in on his name just to experience mediocre investment results?

It was then that I looked back at some of my other investments such as Matex International and I realised what I had been missing out on. It was also then that I realised that my "guru" was Ben Graham and not Warren Buffett. There are many other investment mistakes made along the way but I am not going to bore you with all of them.

As fate and serendipity would have it, I was in no way meant to succeed as an investor buying moated companies at fair prices. However, I believe and I still do that I am meant to be a deep value, net current asset value, Grahamite investor.

Resources at www.theholyfinancier.com

The Holy Financier is an extension of these very books that Kingsley has written. The idea is to use the website as a channel to shed some light on deep value investing and net current asset value investing. If investing in sub-liquidation value stocks is a skill you would like to sharpen, consider accessing www.theholyfinancier.com for a library of:

- **Free articles on investing and life** - Investing is a lifelong process best enjoyed. Be part of our community and share your ideas and thoughts with us.

- Checklist for net current asset value investing - If you are new to the net current asset value strategy, we suggest having a look at our checklist. A checklist ensures to some extent that you are on the right track, making decisions free of most innate biases.

  Scan this QR code to access the checklist:

- **Community** - Join our deep value community! No one knows everything and because investing is such a wide subject, it is always good to be able to share our learnings and our journey. If you ask me, I'd prefer to learn from the vicarious experience of others than my own personal experience. At the same time, humility is an important attribute for learning. Let us share and learn together!

- **Database for net current asset value stocks worldwide** - TheHolyFinancier is essentially a database of net current asset value stocks worldwide. Find net current asset value stocks with ease and at an affordable price.

- **Stock analysis & research** - TheHolyFinancier provides a continuous flow of stock analysis and research for our members.

- **Case studies** - Case studies maketh the investor in our opinion. We are looking for patterns that make for successful investing. We have case studies of failure as well as case studies of success. Each story is unique but the overall patterns are all too similar for the astute investor.

- **Premium articles** - We have some very interesting premium articles that will add to your personal investing journey. Be sure to look out for them!

- How To Research Japanese Stocks? – Learn how to research Japanese stocks and find hidden gems for your portfolio despite the language barriers.

Scan this QR code to research Japanese stocks:

About The Author

Kingsley Lucas is an author, writer and practitioner of deep value investing principles as originally taught by Ben Graham, the father of value investors the world over. Through experience, hard work and some serendipity, he has found that to be a serial compounder in the stock markets, one needs a contrarian mindset that sets himself apart from others. Because at the end of the day, the stock market is just a tool for the transfer of wealth from the misinformed to the informed.

Hence, the question to ask is which side of the investment are you on? Through years of effort and study, Kingsley has found that the number one quality that makes for increased wealth in the stock market is in the curtailment of risk. Once that happens, the upside will naturally take care of itself. If it is one thing that the crowds tend to overlook, it is that mean reversion and its effects can be very substantial and powerful. Mean reversion is the tendency of the prices of stocks to move to a certain average. That also means that baskets of stocks which have been mercilessly beaten down have a tendency rise as a whole.

And as far as Kingsley is concerned, mean reversion is his major catalyst when it comes to the stocks that he purchases. The low prices, in and of themselves, are his primary protection of the downside. And this strategy has served him well. The net current asset value approach is his primary strategy for growing his wealth and the low price to book strategy is an extension of the prior strategy. These stocks and more make up Kingsley's deep value portfolio. He is in every sense of the word, a true blue Grahamite.

Learn more about Kingsley at TheHolyFinancier.com

Also, you can find out more about Kingsley as an author at

http://amazon.com/author/kingsleylucas

OTHER BOOKS BY KINGSLEY

The $20 Million Investor Blueprint: Deep Value Net Current Asset Value Stocks In Japan

The net current asset value strategy is a strategy that works in Japan as well. Japan is a market that has many stocks which Ben Graham would have approved of. Also, investing in net current asset value stocks in Japan means that investors have more opportunities available to them as compared to just investing in the domestic markets. Within this book, the author dives into some case studies that suggest the efficacy of the net current asset value strategy. The case studies also shed light on how net current asset value stocks should be analysed and how to make a basket of such stocks compound money for an investor. The author believes that one is able to grow a portfolio to $20 million with this strategy.

Learn how to:
- How To Mitigate Risk
- Picking Winners
- Taking Advantage Of Dividend Skipping
- How To Earn Up To 300% In Profits

The $20 Million Investor Blueprint: Net Current Asset Value Strategies For The International Investor

This book discusses many case studies of companies on an international basis. The companies mentioned in this book are from UK, Canada, Singapore and Hong Kong. These featured case studies suggest that the net current asset value approach is both feasible and effective in international markets.

For the serious net current asset value investor, this book will be a treasure trove of information. It should also be read with other books such as: The $20 Million Investor Blueprint: Deep Value Net Current Asset Value Stocks In Japan, The $20 Million Investor Blueprint: How Amateur Investors Can Build Their Portfolio To $20 Million and The $20 Million Investor Blueprint: Net Current Asset Value Stocks In The USA.

Reading these books will give investors the conviction that the net current asset value approach does work. The net current asset value strategy can help an investor build a $20 million portfolio over time. If you want to be wealthy, the author's suggestion is to read these books and digest its contents fully.

The $20 Million Investor Blueprint: Net Current Asset Value Stocks In The USA

Benjamin Graham, Walter Schloss, Warren Buffett and Peter Cundill all have one thing in common. They practised the art of buying net current asset value stocks early on in their career.

This book is reveals complete case studies of companies that once traded at less than the calculated net current asset value. It is written for investors who want to invest in the US stock markets or for investors who want to know what to expect from the net current asset value approach. The approach is a methodical way of buying deeply undervalued securities, while maintaining a contrarian view which differs from the market view. As such, many of these stocks do very well. This is a roadmap and blueprint to compounding money at between 20% to 30% per annum.

The Billionaire Investor Blueprint: Low Price To Book Stocks For Tremendous Wealth

The billionaire investor is one who has been able to compound money at high rates over long periods of time. How did they do it? This book is written with the aim of helping investors understand some of the philosophies behind the greatest investors in the world. The low price to book strategy is an overlooked, underused approach in determining a security's undervaluation.

The book contains case studies which many investors will find useful. It is also practical and investors will learn to see the patterns that make for successful investing. This book is an extension of the net current asset value approach.

One Last Thing...

I once had the naïve thought that if I could actually help masses of people to see the "light" when it comes to investing, that would have been my way of enriching the lives of others. I am not sure if I have managed to do that for it is my experience that sometimes, people are not easy to help. These days, I am more realistic. If I can help just a handful of people, I would have considered my mission accomplished.

As far as possible, I have tried to remain in that spirit of "helping" throughout this book. I have bared my heart and my soul within the pages of this book. And I hope that you would take the time to reread this book and to really digest the principles here. Perhaps, you are from another industry and investing concepts may not come easy to you. But given enough time and practice, I believe that you will be able to make a success of this life materially.

I am a big believer in fate and destiny. The stars have decreed that you would be holding onto this very book. What you do with it is entirely up to you! I hope to be able to connect with you in some heartfelt way in the future. The future is yours my dear friend. Do what you will with it!

Make the right choices in life and make the best of life. Remember always that we are part of the divine. And since you are holding onto this book, remember that we are connected in some invisible magical way. If you have found this book useful, do share it with your friends and family. And if you can find it in your heart to leave a review on Amazon, it is much appreciated. Your support means the world to me. I do try to read all the reviews and hope to make improvements to this book to make it better.

If you'd like to leave a review then all you need to do is click the review link on this book's page on Amazon here: https://amzn.to/2KHVRhL

Or scan the QR code below to write a review:

May you be blessed with abundance, wealth, prosperity and all that you need! May you be the best version of yourself! All the best and thank you for the support!

www.ingramcontent.com/pod-product-compliance
Lightning Source LLC
Chambersburg PA
CBHW030015190526
45157CB00016B/2800